Exploring
Printmaking
for Young People

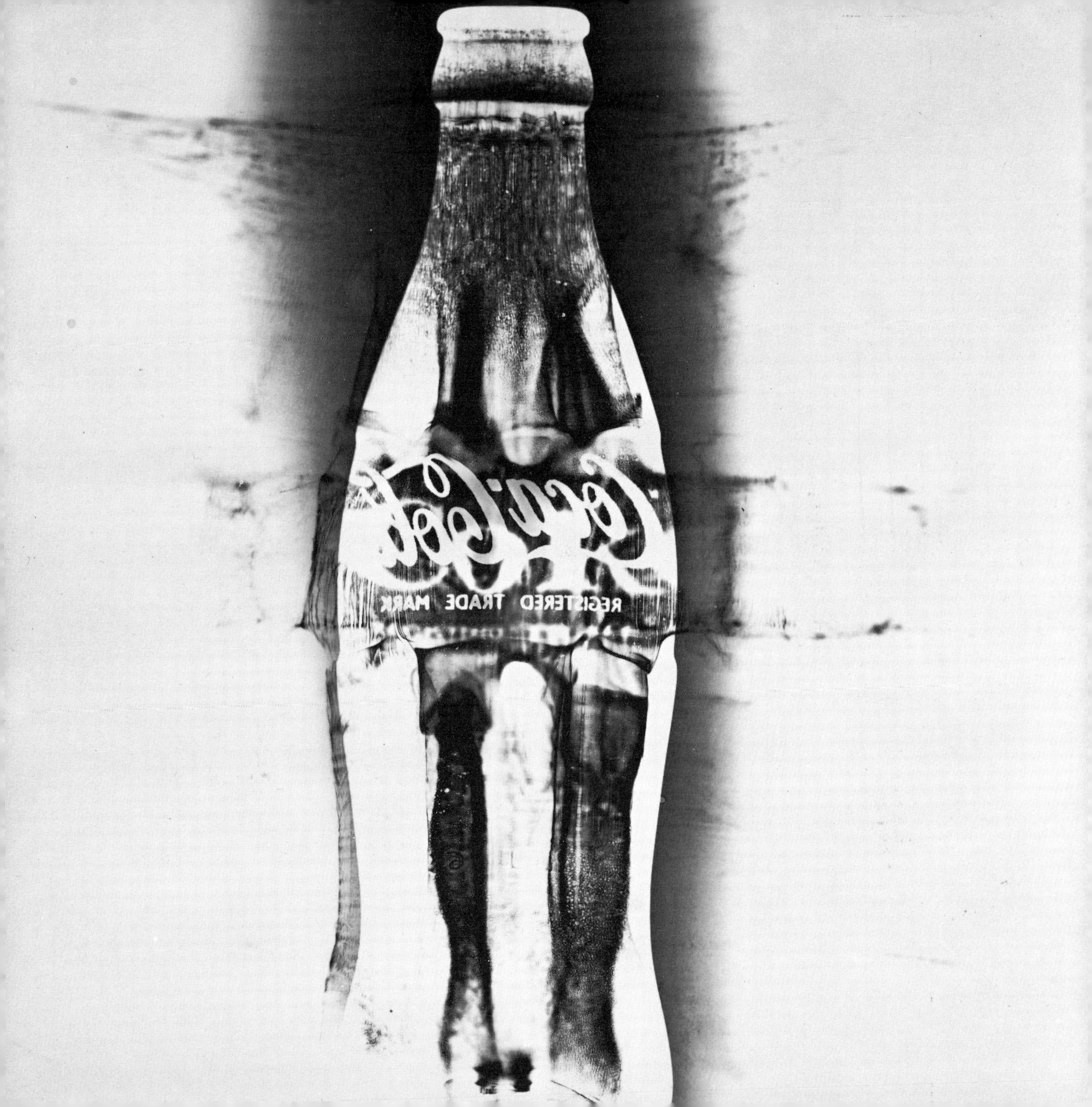
REGISTERED TRADE MARK

Harvey Daniels and Silvie Turner

Exploring Printmaking

for Young People

VNR Van Nostrand Reinhold Company
New York · Cincinnati · Toronto · London · Melbourne

For Arthur Turner

Frontispiece.
'Coca-Cola Bottle'.
Rayogram.

Copyright © Harvey Daniels and
Silvie Turner, 1972.

Library of Congress Catalog
Card Number 72-3542
ISBN 0 442 01987 4

Designed by Rod Josey.
This book is set in Monophoto
Apollo and is printed in Great
Britain by Jolly & Barber Ltd.,
Rugby and bound by the Ferndale
Book Company.

Published by Van Nostrand
Reinhold Company, Inc., 450 West
33rd Street, New York, N.Y. 10001
and Van Nostrand Reinhold
Company Ltd., Windsor House,
25–28 Buckingham Gate, London
SW1.

Published simultaneously in
Canada by Van Nostrand Reinhold
Company Ltd.

16 15 14 13 12 11 10 9 8 7 6 5 4 3 2 1

CONTENTS

INTRODUCTION

Our first book, *Simple Printmaking*, dealt with the easiest methods of making prints. In this book we go further into the printmaking process and explain some of the more complicated print methods. This book is, therefore, more suitable for older children. However, as we said in the first book, many young children do enjoy printmaking using methods that are technically advanced (see Fig. 60), while older children often use very simple methods (see Fig. 44).

Printmaking should be seen as a continuing process of exploration. As John Holt has said in his book *How Children Fail*, 'We cannot have real learning in schools if we think it is our duty and our right to tell children what they must learn.'

To quote John Holt again: 'It is not subject matter that makes some learning more valuable than others, but the spirit in which the work is done. . . . A child who is learning naturally following his curiosity where it leads him is growing in knowledge, in the love of learning and in the ability to learn.'

If we say that this book is aimed at older children it is only because they will be more capable of carrying out a complex research programme within the printmaking media.

Although there are many ways of making prints there are only three basic processes: printing from a raised surface (relief); the reverse of relief, where the print is taken from the lowest surface of the block (intaglio); and printing from a flat surface (planographic).

The first two processes each have a chapter devoted to them, with planographic printing being divided into two chapters, one dealing with lithography and the other with screen-printing. We have also included a chapter on new and mixed media which explores and illustrates some ideas that are not usually accepted as part of the traditional role of printmaking.

However we begin with a brief explanation of printing presses, as most of the methods shown in this book require a press.

Opposite. Fig. 1. Relief print being taken from wooden type on a rotary press by a boy, age 13.

A*

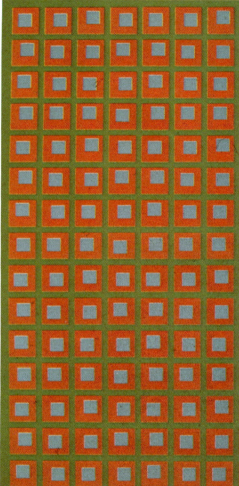

Left. Fig. 2. 'Costa del Sol'.
Mixed media print. Harvey Daniels, Peter
Hawes, Silvie Turner working together.
(Collection D. and J. Smith.)

Right. Fig. 4. 'Moonstrips Empire News,
Formica-Formikel'.
Eduardo Paolozzi, British, born 1924.
This complicated silk-screen print registers
more than fourteen colours. (Courtesy of
the artist.)

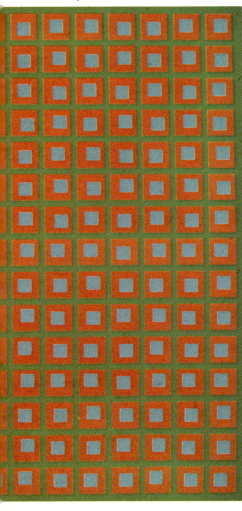

Above. Fig. 3. 'Untitled', 1968.
Phillip Wetton, British, born 1944.
Silk-screen print of bright flat colours.

Below. Fig. 5. 'Plastic Doily'.
Stamp, roller offset and print from inking
up roller. (Imberhorne Comprehensive
School, East Grinstead.)

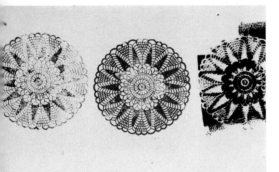

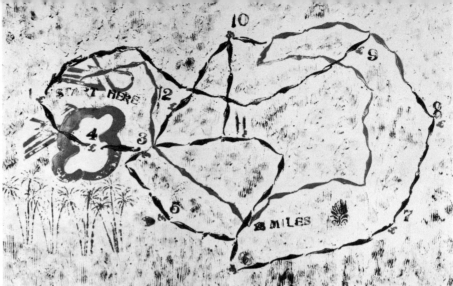

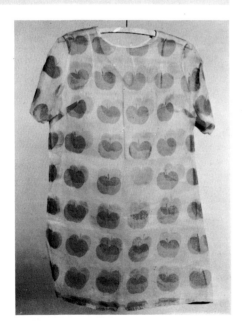

Above. Fig. 6. 'Apple Dress'.
Lizzie Cox, British, born 1946.
Silk-screen print on material. (Brighton
College of Art.)

Above. Fig. 8. Vacuum formed and painted
prints made from actual objects.
D. Susmann, S. Turner. (Brighton College
of Art.)

Above. Fig. 9. Printed tiles designed by
Oliver Williams.

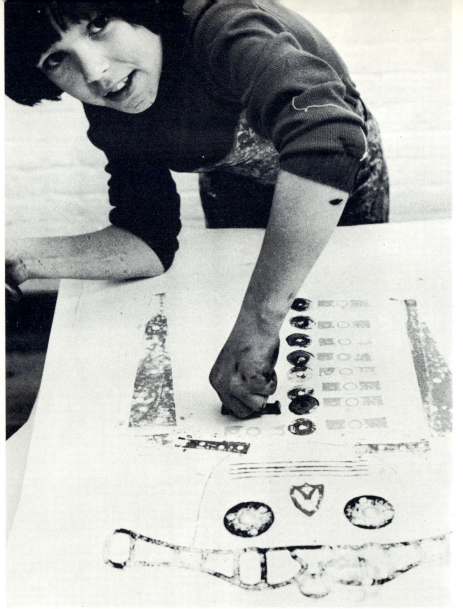

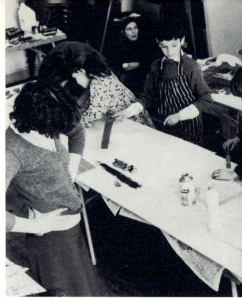

Above. Fig. 10. A stamp print being made.

Top centre. Fig. 11. Children working on three-day printmaking course at County Art Centre, Lewes, Sussex.

Above. Fig. 12. 'My Cat's Name is Puckle'. Ivo Rousham, age 9. Concrete poem. Stamp print and story.

Above. Fig. 14. *Chippenham School Magazine*, 1970.
Silk-screen. Designed, photographed and printed in an edition of 200 by pupils of Chippenham School.

Above. Fig. 13. Emily drawing with her fingers.

Chapter 1
SIMPLE PRINTING PRESSES

Left. Fig. 15. Etching press in use.

Above. Fig. 16. Print being lifted from a cardboard block on an Albion Press.

Any way of applying pressure on to a surface may be called a press, and very often ordinary household objects can be used as presses. The back of a wooden spoon used for burnishing is one very simple press; a large heavy book used to sandwich paper and block (see Fig. 35 in *Simple Printmaking*) is another. Leon Piesowocki uses an ordinary garden roller to print his large relief blocks (see Fig. 23). You can convert a rubber roller into a press by building a box on the handle and filling it with heavy weights, or you can even put a board on top of your block and stamp on it. Possibly the most useful piece of household equipment that can be adapted to print many types of blocks or plates is the old-fashioned mangle or wringer washer (see Fig. 35).

However some forms of print-making do require more sophisticated presses and the use of a press does have certain advantages. A major advantage is the amount of pressure that can be applied. Figs. 25 and 27 show the same object, an egg-box, printed by an Albion press and by hand. The qualities of the two prints are quite different.

The other main advantage of using a press is that by doing so you can repeat the printed image far more quickly and easily as burnishing a large block by hand can be a painstaking and arduous business. Not all the presses mentioned in this chapter are suitable for use in schools. However many can be found in art colleges, workshops or art centres running special classes for children. All the following presses can easily be used in schools: small etching press, small direct litho-proofing press, typewriter, duplicating machine, mangle, hand letterpress machine, pinch or book press, small rotary letterpress machine, Albion press.

Local art colleges and art faculties of universities will often provide help and assistance in locating presses, and may offer part-time facilities for the use of existing presses. Advertisements placed in local trade papers or magazines may be very useful for purchasing unwanted presses inexpensively. If you want to find or buy a press it may well be worth visiting a printing works, especially one which has been recently modernized, as many small presses, formerly used for proofing in industry but now obsolete, may be for sale. These are very adequate for school use.

Operating a press with children,

however, is not without its draw-backs, as will be seen from this description: 'Most of the children considered themselves veterans of the media. Therefore, this time they decided that they wanted to try their strength at running the hand etching press. The first attempt resulted in four boys pulling the arms of the press. With a little additional help we managed to get Aaron's print through the press; the result, however, was a crumpled piece of paper. Mark said we had too much pressure and a dent in the machine. With a little less pressure on the second try we got a good print for Aaron.' (A note made by Melody Weiler, after a Saturday morning class at Ohio University.)

RELIEF PRESSES
The pinch press (Fig. 18) was

formerly used as a bookbinding press. It is very useful for printing small, detailed prints. However, the block must not be too delicate, as the press exerts considerable pressure. As you can see, the press consists of two steel surfaces, one a base, the other a platen, attached to a screw mechanism by which the platen is lowered on to the base, which sandwiches the paper and block together.

The Albion, Washington and Columbian presses work on a more advanced form of the same principle. To operate the press the bed, with the block already inked and the paper in position on it, is wound under the platen and downward pressure is exerted by pulling a handle. The bed is then wound out, the packing or tympan lifted and the print and block removed. Many objects in different

16

colours can be arranged and printed together like this, which is one of the chief advantages of such a press.

There are many smaller hand machines that work on the relief principle. The small hand-operated table model is probably the commonest in use in schools and can print tickets, small magazines and hand-outs. With these machines the leverage of a small handle presses the printing paper against a block of type which is locked into position on a platen.

INTAGLIO PRESSES

An etching press consists of two cylinders of either rubber or metal which are turned by a handle. A metal base, plate, printing paper and packing are forced between the cylinders like washing through a mangle. Because of the tremendous pressure exerted the paper is moulded to the plate, which can be inked or uninked. If it is uninked the impression taken will be a blind embossing.

The best etching press for use in schools is the table model (see Fig. 52). Fig. 15 shows a larger etching press in use. If no etching press is available the best way of printing an etched plate is to use a mangle or wringer roller with soft packing (see Fig. 35).

LITHOGRAPHIC PRESSES

Some types of planographic printing do not require the use of a press, notably stencil printing and silk-screen printing. Lithography does require a press and the simplest type of lithographic press is a small direct proofing press. In these machines a prepared lithographic stone or plate is placed on the bed of the machine and inked. The printing paper and packing are next placed on top of the stone, which is then wound under a scraper bar which forces the ink on to the paper. As in relief printing the image is reversed when printed.

A more sophisticated form of litho printing introduces a rubber roller between the printing plate and the paper. The image is then transferred from the plate on to the rubber roller and from the roller on to the paper. This process, known as offset, produces an identical image to the one appearing on the printing plate. This book is printed by this method.

A small duplicating machine is a form of litho press which can be used in schools.

Above. Fig. 17. 'Two Dams'.
Lynne Moore, British, born 1944.
Cardboard print on Albion press.
(Kemptown Gallery, Brighton.)

18

GENERAL MATERIALS FOR PRINTING

Paper
Newsprint, newspaper, brown wrapping paper, drawing paper, watercolour paper. Smooth paper is most suitable for lithographic printing.

Inks
Oil-based printing inks in tins or tubes; water-based paints or inks.

Rollers
Rubber, composition, plastic.

Mixing and Rolling out Slabs
Glass, marble, lithographic stone, plastic laminate, formica.

Miscellaneous
Workbench or tabletop, wooden spoon, metal spoon, weights, metal rule, string, clothes pegs, drawing pins, Stanley knife, sponge.

Cleaning
Rags, water/soap, white spirit/ turpentine, strong grease cleaner. Consult the list of specialist suppliers on page 86 for material for printing and presses.

Above. Fig. 19. 'Albion press'. Sixth-form pupil. White line lino-cut. (The Art College, Marlborough Boys' School.)

Below. Fig. 21. Lino block ready for printing on bed of Albion press.

Right. Fig. 22. 'Ligatures'.
Stephen Hoare, British, born 1946.
Line of metal type used as a repeat.
Letterpress.

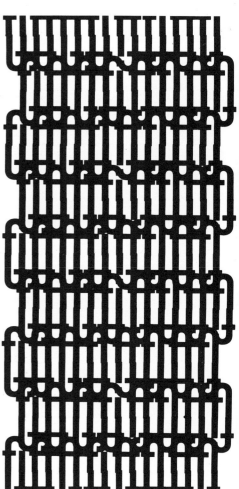

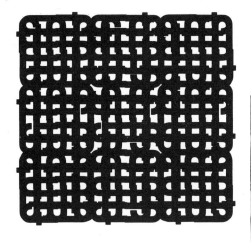

Below. Fig. 25. Egg box printed by hand.
Compare this with Fig. 27.

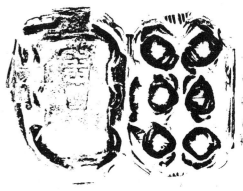

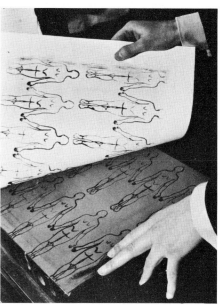

Above. Fig. 26. Print being lifted from
litho plate on direct press.

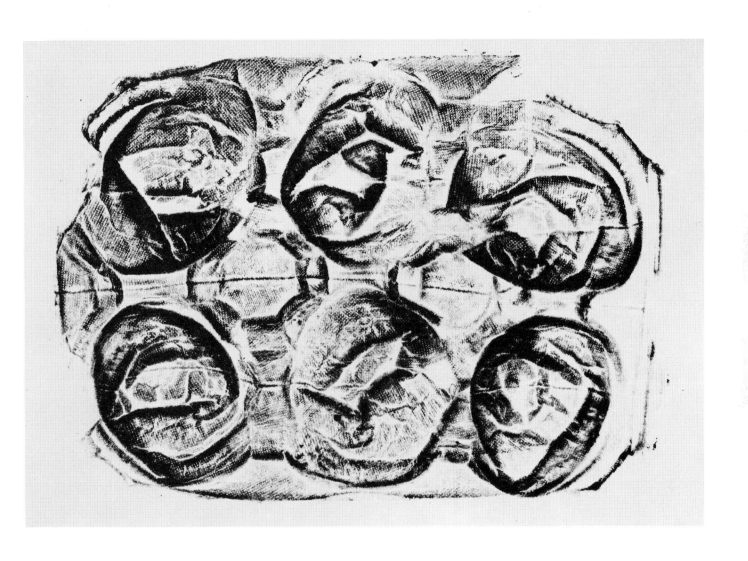

Above. Fig. 27. Flattened egg box printed
in an Albion press.

was speaking, so that her idea of the tale was something
like this:—"Fury said to
a mouse, That
he met in the
house, 'Let
us both go
to law: *I*
will prose-
cute *you.*—
Come, I'll
take no de-
nial: We
must have
the trial;
For really
this morn-
ing I've
nothing
to do.'
Said the
mouse to
the cur,
Such a
trial, dear
sir, With
no jury
or judge,
w o u l d
be wast-
ing our
breath.
'I'll be
judge,
I'll be
jury,
said
cun-
ning
old
Fury:
'I'll
t r y
the
whole
cause,
a n d
con-
demn
you to
death.

"You are not attending!" said the Mouse to Alice,
severely. "What are you thinking of?"

Below. Fig. 29. Booklet cover printed by
duplicating machine, distributed by
Redbridge Art Centre.

Right. Fig. 30. 'A Stitch in Time saves Nine'.
Student. Letterpress. (Bath Academy of
Art. Instructor John Furnival.)

1

st2tch

3n

t4m5

s6v7s

n8n9

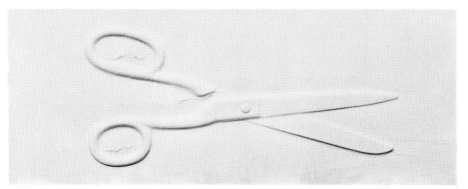

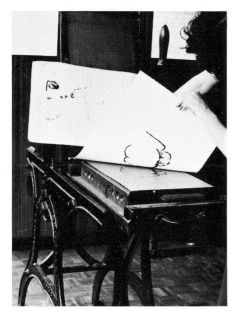

Above. Fig. 32. Direct hand litho press in use.

Above. Fig. 34. 'Air Pollution Problem'. Jeffrey Stewart, age 12. Lino-cut cartoon, printed on an etching press. (Saturday morning children's class, Ohio University. Instructor Melody Weiler.)

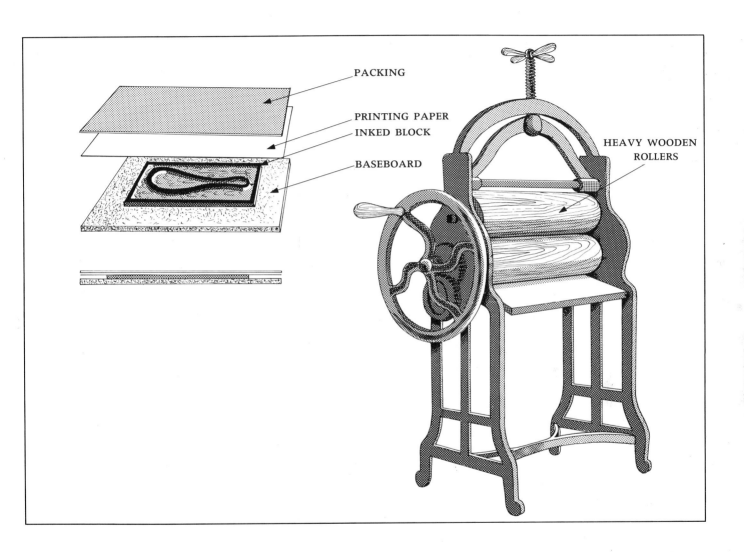

PACKING

PRINTING PAPER

INKED BLOCK

BASEBOARD

HEAVY WOODEN
ROLLERS

Above. Fig. 35. Diagram of a mangle or
wringer roller showing block, paper,
packing and boards.

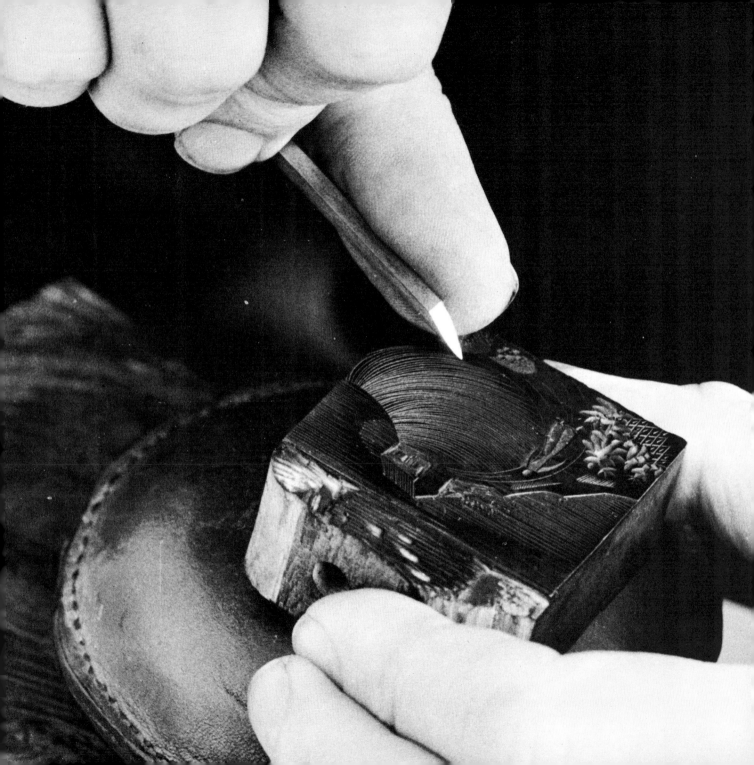

Chapter 2
RELIEF PRINTING
IN COLOUR

In the relief process the print is
taken from the top surface of a
block which has been inked. It
includes lino printing, wood
engraving, cardboard printing and
complex surface printing of all
types.

In this chapter we have concentrated on ways of printing
colour. Although some of the
methods described are not
commonly used they are neverthe-
less suitable for use by children
of all ages. A press is a great
advantage here but any adaptation
of the relief process, for instance
the pinch press, can be used
successfully.

Relief printing enables a
collection of objects or surfaces to
be assembled and printed quickly
and efficiently at the same time.
This means that children can easily
assemble complex pages of visual
information. However, as mentioned
in the companion volume, *Simple
Printmaking*, if collections of
objects are being printed together
you should make sure that the
objects are of similar height.

Three-dimensional objects can
be printed in a relief press (see Figs.
27 and 50). They can be flattened
or alternatively a different print
can be taken from each surface. If
this is done then the image of the
object can be reassembled from the
various prints (see Fig. 49).

Relief printing, especially with
cardboard, is an excellent way for
children to use and experience
colour. They can cut out a
design from a piece of cardboard,
ink the separate pieces in different
colours and then fit them together
like a jig-saw puzzle, to be printed
together.

Alternatively they can ink one

piece of cardboard with three bright colours and print them together so that they merge in a rainbow of bright colours. Another plan is to experiment with one colour, using different pigments (for instance oil- and water-based paint), overprinting, printing large and small areas. This can lead to other colour experiments and provides a direct link with the science of colour.

MATERIALS AND TOOLS
Relief Printing
Found objects such as scissors, tin cans, car parts, clothing, or blocks such as lino or wood.
Rollers.
Coloured inks, oil- or water-based.
Tracing paper.
Relief printing press.
Packing material, blankets or news-sheet.

Tissue paper, absorbent paper, weights.
Cardboard Printing
Scalpel or Stanley (exacto) knife.
Smooth-quality cardboard. Tracing or carbon paper. Cutting surface.

HOW TO MAKE BLOCKS
Found Objects
If necessary, any found objects should be cleaned before you start printing. Collect together the the objects you wish to print. These objects can be mounted on a base for accuracy of arrangement if you intend to take a number of prints. In order to seal the surface, roll a layer of ink over the object surface and leave it to dry.
As described in *Simple Printmaking*, there are many ways of creating your own blocks.
Cardboard Blocks
(The same method may be applied to hardboard, thin wood, metal or acrylic.) You can draw on to the cardboard directly, taking care to reverse an already made drawing if the printed image is wanted the correct way round. This can be done by using carbon paper and tracing paper.

Cut out the drawn shapes with a sharp knife, scalpel or stencil knife. If you have cut the shapes from a drawing on cardboard with a Stanley (exacto) knife or thick cutting blade white lines will be left round each shape when printed, because of the thickness of the cutting blade. If areas of close-fitting colour are wanted, shape must be traced and cut out separately, using a key or registration sheet as a guide.

INKING UP
Roll the ink out evenly on to a

Fig. 38. Registration method for cardboard colour blocks on Albion press.

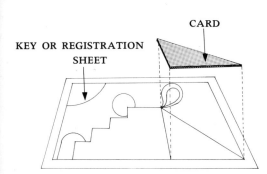

KEY OR REGISTRATION SHEET

CARD

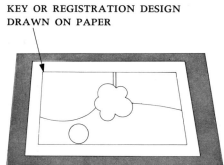

KEY OR REGISTRATION DESIGN DRAWN ON PAPER

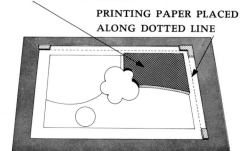

ONE PIECE OF INKED CARDBOARD PLACED ON REGISTRATION SHEET

PRINTING PAPER PLACED ALONG DOTTED LINE

clean smooth surface. Roll a film of ink over the top surface of the block/object. The texture of the ink should be tacky, although this should be related to the absorbency of the object.

When you are inking paper and cardboard blocks mix some linseed oil with the ink. This prevents it being too tacky, since otherwise the top layer of cardboard will peel off. Too much ink on the block causes a soft, sloppy edge when printed, whereas insufficient ink on the block causes an overall texture on the print.

RELIEF PRINTING
Before printing adjust the pressure of the press to suit the block height. Decide on the position of the objects to be printed and then mark their outlines on a sheet of

tracing paper. This is called the registration sheet and is placed on the base of the press. Then place the inked-up objects in the appropriate positions, lay the printing paper on top of them and mark its position on the registration sheet if you are going to take more than one print. Next place the blanket and/or packing on top of the printing paper. Remember that if you use hard packing you will print the top surface of the block only, while soft packing allows a deeper surface to be printed. It is essential to use smooth paper, as rough-surfaced paper will not usually take a flat colour.

CARDBOARD PRINTING
Ink each piece of cardboard separately and assemble all of them

in the correct position on the registration sheet (see Fig. 43). Take the print as described above.
Stripping
If too much ink has been deposited on the paper during printing, you can blot the print with absorbent tissue to remove the surplus. This can be done either by hand or in a press.

COLOUR MERGE OR RAINBOW PRINTING (See Fig. 40)
Place two different colours of ink, for example red and yellow, at either side of the rolling-up slab. Merge the inks by continually rolling up and down the slab with a clean roller until red merges with yellow, making orange in the centre of the roller. You may need to move the roller slightly sideways to help to begin the blend.

Above. Fig. 40. Cardboard block being rolled up with three-colour merge.

Left. Fig. 42. 'Rocket U.S.A.'.
Bobby Betz III, age 8. Single colour lino print. (Saturday morning children's class, Ohio University. Instructor Melody Weiler.)

Below. Fig. 44. 'Letter E'.
Foundation student, age 19. Bath Academy of Art. Colour cardboard print, showing merge. In this print colour was used to give a three-dimensional illusion.

Right. Fig. 45. 'Harley Davidson'.
Lino cut made in a children's class at Ohio University.

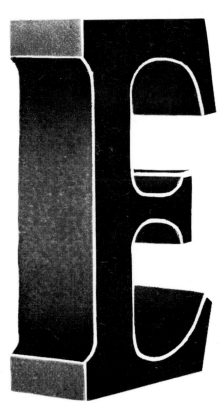

Above. Fig. 43. Rolled up coloured shapes of cardboard being assembled on registration sheet.

Above. Fig. 46. Cardboard print being lifted from coloured cardboard blocks on Albion press by Debora Sumpter, age 12.

Below. Fig. 47. 'Look for the White Birdie',
1963. Michael Rothenstein, British, born
1908. Block print. The artist uses found
materials in his prints (in this instance a
piece of wood). (Courtesy of the artist.)

Fig. 48. 'Circle 2'.
Pat Thornton, British, born 1946.
Cardboard print with merge.

Below. Fig. 49. 'Telephone'.
A three-dimensional relief print which was made from the separate parts of a telephone and then assembled as a paper representation.

Bottom left. Fig. 50. Three-dimensional relief print from tin can. Foundation-year student. (Brighton Polytechnic. Instructors Pat Thornton, Trevor Allen.)

Below. Fig. 51. 'Mickey Mouse'. Carol Hamling, age 15. Cardboard print.

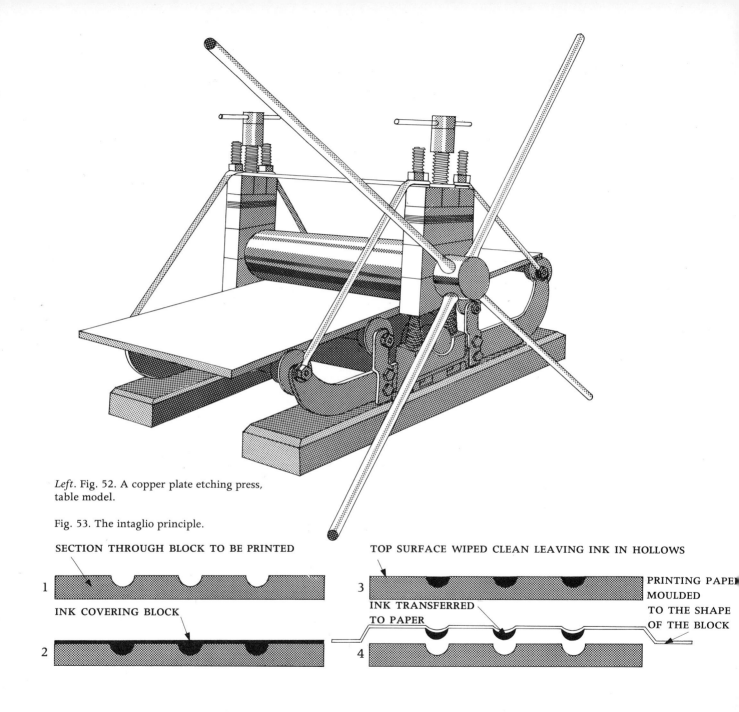

Left. Fig. 52. A copper plate etching press, table model.

Fig. 53. The intaglio principle.

SECTION THROUGH BLOCK TO BE PRINTED

TOP SURFACE WIPED CLEAN LEAVING INK IN HOLLOWS

1

3

PRINTING PAPER
MOULDED
TO THE SHAPE
OF THE BLOCK

INK COVERING BLOCK

INK TRANSFERRED
TO PAPER

2

4

Chapter 3
INTAGLIO PRINTING

'On objects of horn, of bone, and of stone, as on the walls of caves decorated by palaeolithic man, incised lines accompany and may even predate drawn and painted images.' *William Hayter*.

In intaglio an impression is taken from the lower levels of the plate or block, the top surface of which has been wiped clean. The technique was first introduced with the decoration of armour by hammering, etching and engraving, the traditional intaglio print being taken from a metal plate on which a variety of marks had been made.

The differences between the processes of relief and intaglio are not in the blocks or plates but in the method of printing. Fig. 31 shows a print of a pair of scissors where the impression has been taken by the intaglio method, but uninked. This process is called 'embossing' and is a very simple introduction to the intaglio process.

The etching of plates with acid is the one intaglio process involving a chemical change. When etched, the marks on the plate change their character completely. Because of the thickness of the etching plate and the use of dampened paper to print with, intaglio is almost the only method in which a print is moulded to the shape of the plate. And because the metal is tough and rigid, the prints have a certain strength and authority.

Each method of making a plate is completely different, showing a great change in the printed result. No other medium will print a sharper, more incised line than if a hard, acid-resistant ground has been drawn into an etched plate (see Fig. 60).

Above. Fig. 54. Heavy mangle with wooden rollers.

It is possible to impress a texture of almost any material on to the plate by using a soft ground. This is then made permanent by etching it on to the plate (see Fig. 62).

Although traditionally intaglio prints are made in black and white, it is possible to use colour in etching. Many artists now practise a method developed by William Hayter, who uses the viscosity of the inks to separate the different colours on different levels of the plate. Figs. 65 and 67 show a photograph of an etched plate and a print taken from it in four colours. The print was made by putting black and violet into the lower levels of the plate by the intaglio method, then rolling yellow and blue on to the top surface of the plate. The four-colour plate was put through the press in one printing.

It is very easy to print a two-colour etching by simplifying Hayter's principle, inking the lowest levels of the plate in one colour and rolling up the surface of the plate in another. Different ways of printing more than one colour on the plate include stencilling on to the plate with simple paper stencils, or rolling up different parts of the plate by hand, with different colours on separate rollers.

Children enjoy the involvement of such a traditional way of printing. There is a long craftsman-like preparation of the metal plate, followed by a great deal of satisfaction at seeing the print lifted off the etching plate. Many teachers have regarded etching as a dull, laborious method of working. This is not so. With the method known as drypoint, a print can be made from a plate which has been incised but not etched. Metals can be shaped, bent, hammered and punched, or other materials such as celluloid, lucite or plastic can be gouged or engraved quite easily with a vibro or other hand-machine tool. In addition, the plates themselves can be used in many constructive and exciting ways, for example rolled in flat colour and printed in relief.

Some of the prints in this chapter, for example 'House and Garden' (Fig. 60), have not been processed or printed by the children themselves. However, it is possible for even young children to make a celluloid drypoint which they can then print themselves in intaglio, using a small table model etching press or a mangle with a hardboard bed, and thick blankets.

Below. Fig. 56. An intaglio print and a
blind embossed print of a plastic comb.

Bottom. Fig. 57. Etching studio.

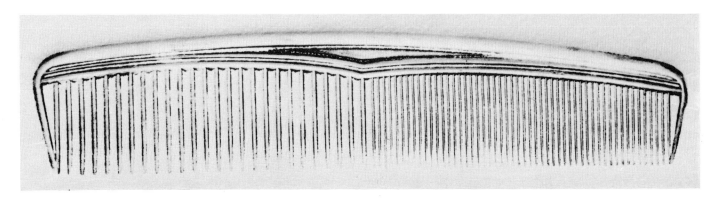

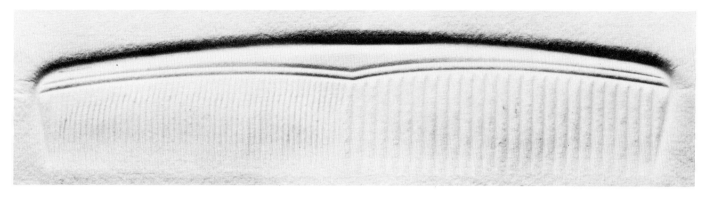

All the methods of making an intaglio print have certain aspects in common, the most typical being the three-dimensional quality of the printed image. All the sculptural qualities of an object or plate can be reproduced in a moulded form (see Fig. 56). This method of printing allows the outside shape of an object or plate to take precedence and provides a link with the three-dimensional, sculptural aspect of printing.

MATERIALS AND TOOLS
Plates
Metal: *copper, zinc, iron, steel.*
Plastics: *celluloid, lucite, plexiglass, perspex.*
Steel guillotine, hacksaw or draw tool.
Etching press.
Etching blankets.

Acids
Nitric acid. (Appropriately diluted, this is a good all-purpose acid for steel, zinc and iron but is not recommended for copper plates unless the room is well ventilated, as the reaction between copper and nitric acid gives off poisonous fumes.)
Acid baths of porcelain, enamel or acid-proof plastic.
Glass storage jars for acid.
Feathers.
Glass funnels.

Tools
Engraving tools, etching needles, burin and drypointing tools.
Hand-power tools (see Fig. 61).
Scraper/burnisher. Charcoal. Oil.
Hard-ground/soft-ground ball. Ink.
Ink slab. Thin, medium and stiff oil – i.e. grease. A hot plate. Muslin, cheesecloth, scrim or tarlatan.

Printing paper. Tissue paper, news-sheet. French chalk, ammonia, silver polish.

HOW TO MAKE PLATES
Preparation
Clean the plates before beginning work on them. You can remove light scratches by burnishing with charcoal and light oil, dirt with silver polish and grease with French chalk and ammonia. Take care to handle the cleaned plates at their edges only.
Drypoint
The design is scratched on to the plate by means of a drypoint tool or any thin, sharp instrument. Traditionally, copper plate is used for this method, but many plastics (e.g. lucite, plexiglass, celluloid) give excellent results.
Engraving
An engraving is made with a burin.

Again traditionally made on copper, engravings are now made on many other materials. Hold the tool as for engraving a piece of wood (see Fig. 36). In engraving, a curl of metal is cut out of the plate with the pressure exerted by the hand, the depth of the line depending on the pressure exerted. To make a curved line move the plate, not the tool. You can use a multiple tool to engrave a number of lines at the same time.

Etching

Cover the back and sides of the plate with an acid resist (e.g. stopping-out varnish), as any parts that are not covered are eaten away when the plate is put into the acid. For a hard-ground resist melt a small amount of the ball ground on to the surface of a gently heated clean plate, and roll it evenly over the plate, away from the heat, with a hard roller.

You can smoke the plate with a lighted taper to blacken it so that, as the drawing proceeds, the lines on the plate can be seen easily. The blackened hard ground forms a smooth, tough surface. This method is used for fine line drawings where accurate detail is needed (see Fig. 64).

For a soft-ground resist roll the wax over the plate as above. The plate is not smoked and the wax is more impressionable than the hard-ground resist. You can press textures or impressions from objects into it (for example, feathers, grass or hands) (see Fig. 62). When you have finished drawing or impressing your design on to the plate it can then be put in the acid bath.

Prepare the acid bath with roughly one part nitric acid to three parts water. Stronger mix-tures can be used but you should take care that they do not lift the ground off the plate in the early stages of biting. *Always* pour the acid into the water, since water added to acid causes an explosion, and avoid or disperse the fumes made by any plate that has large areas of metal exposed.

During the biting period the acid will weaken, so the mixture should be strengthened by adding more acid. It is not possible to give accurate biting times for plates, particularly those with large areas exposed, as this depends on the acid-weakening factor and also on the temperature. Action is quicker at higher temperatures.

Keep exposed areas of the plate free from nitric oxide bubbles by moving the bubbles with a feather, as these retard the biting process. Any ground that comes off the

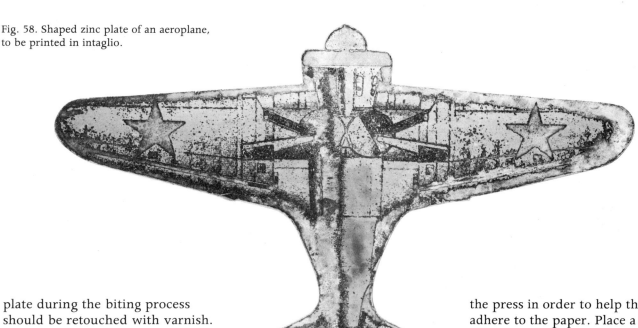

plate during the biting process should be retouched with varnish. When the plate has been bitten deeply enough remove it from the bath with wooden tongs and wash it thoroughly under running water. If at any time any acid gets splashed on to your skin wash it off thoroughly and immediately.

The wax and varnish can then be removed with turpentine and the etching plate is ready for inking and printing.

INKING UP THE BLOCK OR PLATE

The edges of all plates must be bevelled, or filed at an angle of 45°, after work on them has been completed, as otherwise the plate will cut through both the printing paper and the blanket when wound through the press.

Warm the plate slightly and cover it with ink, using a pad or dabber. All recesses in the plate must be filled with ink. Remove the surface ink with a pad of soft muslin, scrim or tarlatan, rotating the plate continually while wiping to prevent the ink from being lifted out of the recesses. Remove any further ink from the surface of the plate with tissue or newspaper and, if necessary, wipe gently with the side of the hand. Finally, wipe the edges of the plate clean.

PRINTING

The plate must be warmed slightly before it is put on to the bed of the press in order to help the ink adhere to the paper. Place a sheet of damp paper carefully on top of the plate. Lay a sheet of tissue paper and the etching blankets smoothly and carefully over the plate and paper. Run the metal bed through the press by turning the wheel. As the dampened paper passes through the cylinders it is pressed on to the metal plate. Throw the blankets back and lift the print carefully off the plate (see Fig. 63). As the print is damp it should be covered with tissue or blotting paper and placed between heavy boards. This will protect it and also keep it flat while it is drying.

CLEANING

All the ink must be removed from the recesses of the plate before it is put away.

Below. Fig. 59. 'Bookmarker'.
Chris Bryant, age 16. Hard-ground line
etching.

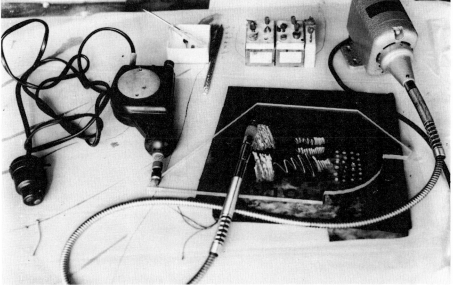

Above. Fig. 60. 'House and Garden'.
Emma Hadley, age 5. Hard-ground line
etching. This print was not processed by
the child.

Above. Fig. 61. Various drills and a sheet of
shaped perspex that has been worked on
by hand-power tools.

Above. Fig. 62. 'Plimsolls'.
Silvie Turner, British, born 1946. Relief
print, with eyelets and laces, taken from
soft-ground etching plates that were shaped
after they had been left in a slow acid
bath. The character of the tennis pumps
was reproduced by impressing them into
the soft ground.

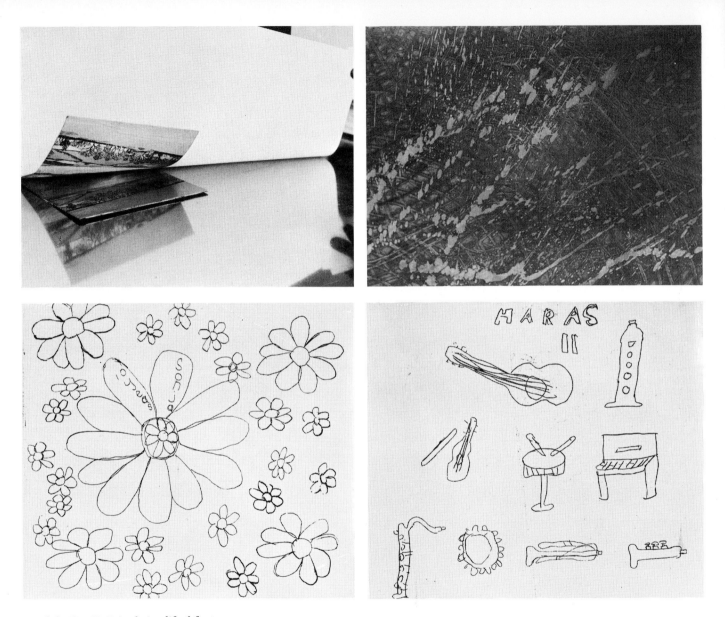

Top left. Fig. 63. Print being lifted from an etching plate.

Above left. Fig. 64. 'Flowers'. Sonja Hadley, age 10. Hard line etching.

Top right. Fig. 65. The etching plate, used in Fig. 67.

Above. Fig. 66. 'Musical Instruments'. Sarah Hadley, age 11. Hard-ground line etching, using a nail as a tool.

Fig. 67. 'Pelagic Forms'.
William Hayter, British, born 1928.
Colour etching. (Courtesy of the Victoria
and Albert Museum.)

Chapter 4
LITHOGRAPHY

Left. Fig. 68. 'Mary and Stephen/Mum and Dad'. Janet Suckling, age 14. Litmask, four-colour stencil made on offset litho press.

The principle of lithography is based on the fact that water and grease do not mix. A litho plate or stone is treated so that some parts will accept grease (printing ink) and repel water while the remainder of the plate or stone will accept water and repel grease.

This chapter serves only as an introduction to the principles of lithography, the methods described involving only basic materials and simple ways of taking prints; it does not deal with complicated colour registration and printing.

When printing a litho plate you must roll it with water first and then with ink, before passing it through the press. As explained in Chapter 1, direct litho reverses the image while offset litho prints the image as it appears on the plate. Many small direct lithographic presses have been installed in

schools and we have found that children have mastered the principles of direct printing very quickly.

Children often find it rewarding to see the result of their own work at the end of a long technical process. We have seen children who have worked on a block for a considerable length of time jumping with excitement waiting for a print to come off the press, and being delighted with the result.

If the technical problems of processing and printing a litho plate – which are complicated rather than difficult – can be overcome, the making of a plate and printing of a lithograph is extremely simple. Children can draw directly on to a plate or stone using litho chalk, crayon, ink or any greasy material. A child may feel less inhibited when mak-

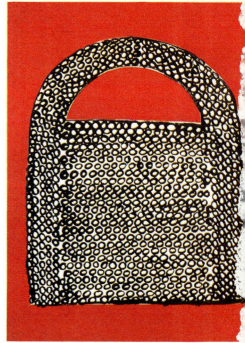

Above. Fig. 69. 'Benzo Moteur Essence Spéciale Pour Automobiles'. J. Chéret, French, 1836–1933. Lithographic poster. (Courtesy of the Victoria and Albert Museum. © by S.P.A.D.E.M., Paris 1971.)

Top right. Fig. 70. 'Tri-Colour Overprint'. Kerith Mackenzie. Lithograph. A particular characteristic of lithography is the over-printing of colours. In this print a variety of colour combinations was made by over-printing red, yellow and blue in different places.

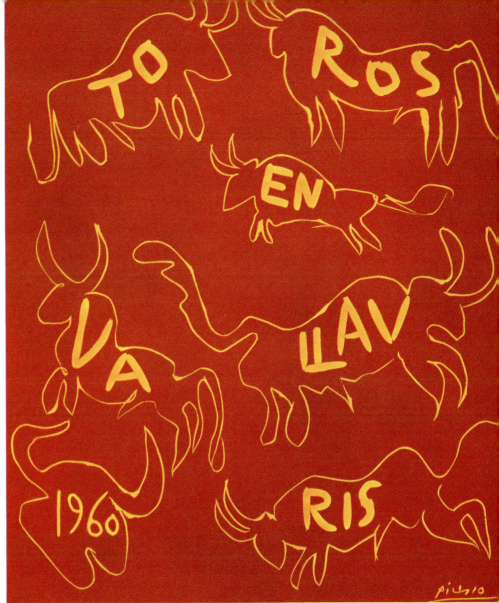

Left. Fig. 71. 'Bead Bags', 1970.
Harvey Daniels, British, born 1936.
Litho and Litmask.

Above. Fig. 72. 'Toros en Vallauris'.
Pablo Picasso, Spanish, born 1881.
Lithographic poster. (© by S.P.A.D.E.M.,
Paris 1971.)

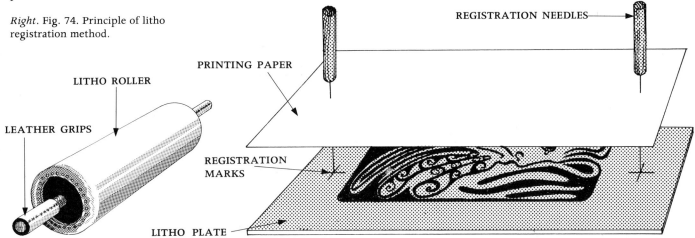

Left. Fig. 73. Small direct lithographic press in use.

Right. Fig. 74. Principle of litho registration method.

REGISTRATION NEEDLES

PRINTING PAPER

LITHO ROLLER

LEATHER GRIPS

REGISTRATION MARKS

LITHO PLATE

ing a lithograph because of the direct contact with drawing, as opposed to a more mechanical technique such as lino-cutting or etching, and may, therefore feel free to express himself by simply drawing or writing on the plate.

It is possible to re-use each plate or stone many times by erasing the drawn image and resensitizing the plate to accept grease. For young children a simpler method is available in which stones or plates are not necessary. Paper lithographic plates need minimal processing and do not necessitate the use of a press; they are therefore very adaptable for school use.

Possibly the most practical aspect of lithography in schools is the chance it gives children to produce posters, broadsheets and small books, as it is technically possible to take large numbers of

prints from the same plate because the image does not deteriorate with printing.

HOW TO MAKE A LITHO PLATE

Preparation
Any marks left on the plate from greasy hands will subsequently print and to prevent this you should gum the plate for approximately 1 inch around the edge. The plate is then ready for drawing on with grease. Either draw directly with a greasy substance on to the plate or transfer an already drawn image by using carbon paper. Remember to draw the image in reverse if a direct printing press is being used.

Processing
Brief instructions on processing plates are given in Fig. 81. The

gum is gum arabic, which is used as an agent to desensitize the plate to grease. Asphaltum, being a grease, reinforces the greasy image during processing.

Inking up the plate
Roll the colour out smoothly on an ink slab with a composition roller. Damp the plate with water sponge and roll it up with the desired colour. The plate must be redamped and rolled after each printing.

MATERIALS AND TOOLS

Drawing
Ruling pens, brushes, litho ink, crayon or any object that makes a greasy mark (e.g. lipstick, candle, polish pad); gum arabic, gum sponges, non-greasy red carbon paper.

Processing
Resin and French chalk, water

D*

Below. Fig. 75. 'Dinosaurs'. Michael Snavely, age 7. Lithograph. The method of drawing on the plate is very simple. The print shows a characteristic of the lithograph in which the marks reproduced are not transformed by the technique in any way but are printed exactly as they were drawn.

Below. Fig. 77. 'Ants'. Group lithograph by children, age 7–12. The group involvement was spontaneous and started from one boy's drawing on a large stone. This attracted the curiosity of the other children and, working on different areas of the stone, they put down their own ideas. There is no question of the print being looked at 'the right way up'!

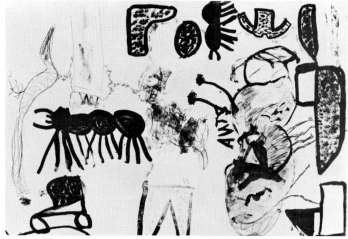

Above. Fig. 76. 'Group Lithograph'. This was made by children, age 5–13, using a variety of drawing materials.

Above. Fig. 78. 'Head'. Michael Snavely, age 7. Lithograph, showing the gestural marks which this method invites. (Saturday morning children's class, Ohio University. Instructor Melody Weiler.)

Below. Figs. 79 and 80. 'Vital Statistics'.
Elena Thompson. Litmask stencil in three
colours. A stencil was made for each colour.
'Female, age 14, 34-28-36, height 5' 1",
eyes green'. Rubbing.

In these two illustrations visual equiva-
lents were found for information which
concerned the girl herself. The 'beauty' of
the print is irrelevant.

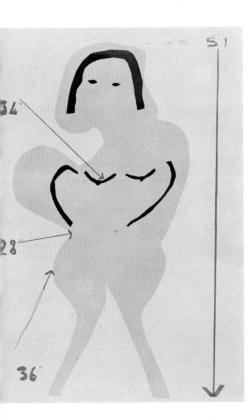

bucket, water sponges, lithographic
etch, small decorator's brush, gum
cloth, fans, rolling-up slabs, non-
drying black proofing ink, nap
rollers, leather grips, matchsticks,
pumice, turpentine/white spirit,
asphaltum, clean white rag, erasing
solution, resensitizing solution.

Printing
Press (some firms make presses
that will print both litho and
etching plates – e.g. the Dickerson
Combination Press); *zinc plates,
paper plates or litho stones;
composition rollers, offset litho inks,
paper packing, thick and thin varnish,
dryers, registration needles.*

PRINTING

Direct Press
Fan the plate dry before each
printing. Place the plate on the bed
of the press and lay the paper
carefully on top. Lower the packing
and tympan on top of the printing
paper. Push the bed of the press a
short way in and lock it in
position with a lever. Turn the
handle to wind the bed of the
press under the scraper bar. This
presses down on the plate and the
image is transferred directly on to
the paper. The printed image is
reversed.

Offset Press
The image on the plate is picked up
by a rubber roller and transferred
from there to the paper surface.
The print on the paper is the same
way round as the image drawn on
to the plate. (Fig. 89 shows an
offset press and the transference of
an image on to paper by a roller.)

COLOUR PRINTING
A plate to be printed in colour is

1	[diagram: gum block, plate]	Gum approx 1" around edge of plate. Gum about 3" on one of longer sides if plate is to be used on offset press — 1" as normal for other sides
2	[diagram: bottle, chalk, plate, flames]	Draw design in grease litho chalk, liquid litho ink, boot polish etc. Dry - some heat may be used
3	[diagram: FRENCH CHALK tin]	Dust lightly with French chalk to prevent smudging
4	[diagram: block, plate]	Gum plate and dry
5	[diagram: block, sponge, plate]	Soften up with gum sponge and reduce to thin film by rubbing down and smoothing with gum cloth. Dry
6	[diagram: bottle, plate]	Wash out design with white spirit using dry clean rag. Dry
7	[diagram: A bottle, pad, plate]	Asphaltum with pad. Rub down to smooth film with clean rag. Dry
8	[diagram: block]	Remove asphaltum with water, sponging gently until image appears brown. Wash out sponge
9	[diagram: block, roller, plate]	Remove surplus water with sponge and reduce to damp even film and then alternately rolling and damping charge plate with black. Dry when image sufficiently black
10	[diagram: RESIN tin, FRENCH CHALK tin, block]	Dust plate with resin and French chalk. Wipe off with sponge.
11	[diagram: PUMICE tin, block, plate]	On wet plate clean up using pumice powder + damp felt - sponge off. Dry.
12	[diagram: ETCH tin, brush, block, plate]	Etch for ½ - 1½ mins., brushing round edges first + keep moving over plate. Wash off with sponge. Wash back of plate + stone. Wash etch from sponge. Dry
13	[diagram: block, cloth, plate]	Gum plate + reduce to thin film with gum cloth. Dry
14	[diagram: bottle, A bottle, block, roller]	Prepare for printing by washing out work with white spirit and asphaltum, reducing both to thin film. Wash with sponge. Damping + rolling — black, white or colour.

New plate handled by edges — Grease from fingers will print on sensitized plate

Left. Fig. 81. Litho broadsheet explaining how to process a plate.

Below. Fig. 82. 'Alphabet in the Form of an Ice Cream Bar', 1970.
Claes Oldenburg, American, born 1929.
Lithographic poster. (Courtesy of the artist.)

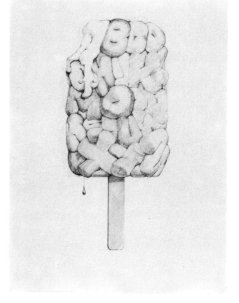

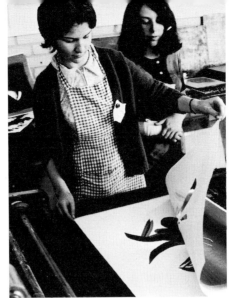

Right. Fig. 84. Litmask or paper stencil
being printed on an offset press.

Below. Fig. 83. Edition of 'litho print drying'.

drawn and processed in the usual way (see Fig. 81). When printing, coloured ink is used to roll up the image. A print in many different colours will need a separate plate for each part of the colour design. One colour should be completely dry before the next is printed on top. A careful tracing of the design is transferred to the plate by the use of red carbon paper. This helps to ensure the correct positioning or registration of subsequent colours. To facilitate the accurate positioning or registration of colours, special registration marks can be made on the top and bottom of each plate. These must be in the same place in relation to the design each time. For each subsequent colour the paper is pinned on to these marks (see Fig. 74).

LITMASK OR LITHO STENCILS

A small offset press is ideal for printing paper stencils. Cut or tear a design out of paper, thus making a stencil. Place the stencil over the printing paper. The coloured ink is then rolled out evenly over the whole area of a smooth litho plate. This colour is then transferred to the roller, which passes over the mask and the printing paper. (Fig. 84 shows an offset stencil print being made.)

Left. Fig. 86. Offset roller print of a spanner.

Bottom left. Fig. 87. 'Get those Dirty Feet off my Ceiling'.
Gary Paudler, age 11. Lithograph.
(Saturday morning children's class, Ohio University. Instructor Melody Weiler.)

Below. Fig. 88. Detail from 'Landscape'.
Jeffrey Stewart, age 12. Lithograph. This shows the sensitivity of drawing on a litho plate. (Saturday morning children's class, Ohio University. Instructor Melody Weiler.)

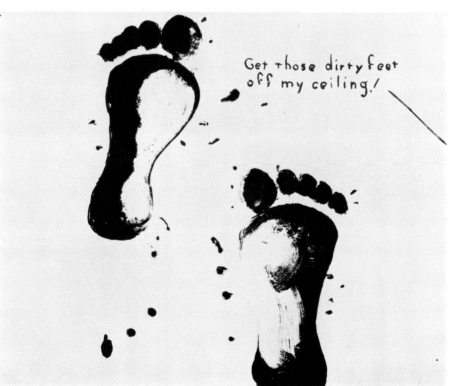

Right. Fig. 89. Offset press showing the design which has been transferred from the plate to the roller, being printed on to the paper. On this sort of press it is possible to make simple flat-colour prints using a paper stencil.

Bottom right. Fig. 90. Paper stencil for a Litmask print being cut out.

Chapter 5
SCREEN PRINTING

Left. Fig. 91. 'Liquorice Allsorts'. Hospital ward project for children. Paper stencil silk-screen. (Newton Park College. Instructor David Andrews.)

Screen printing, another planographic process, is a development of stencil printing. Very simply a mesh made of silk, organdie or nylon is stretched tightly over a frame. A stencil is placed below the mesh with the printing paper underneath and ink is forced through the mesh and on to the paper by a squeegee being pulled across the surface of the mesh.

As this printing method does not require a printing press it is very suitable for children. Silk-screen, the term by which this process is generally known has become very sophisticated and mechanized and is used in industry for printing wallpapers, tiles, fabrics, carpets and containers. It is also used by many artists (see Fig. 100).

The easiest way to make a stencil is to cut or tear a design in a sheet of paper. This is an ideal process for very young children. At the other end of the scale older children can make photographic stencils – a process outside the scope of this book. We have concentrated on fairly simple methods of stencil making, but even these can produce results of great variety and visual impact.

The main advantages of screen printing lie in the variety of inks that can be used and the speed of printing. It is possible to use transparent, gloss, matt and fluorescent inks, and this is the only method where white can be printed on top of black and remain white. If you use inks which dry quickly you can print as many as four colours in a day and take a considerable number of prints as well (see Fig. 94). This can be very useful if you want to print posters

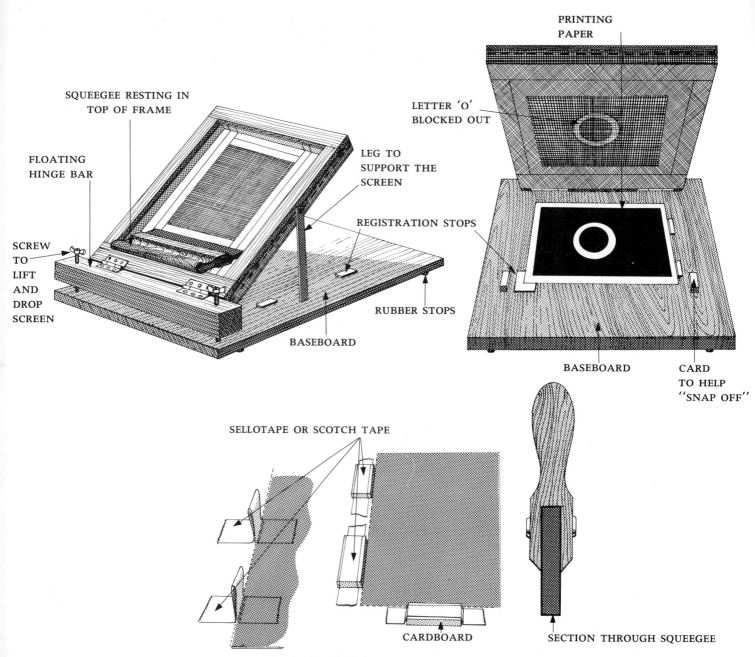

SQUEEGEE RESTING IN
TOP OF FRAME

FLOATING
HINGE BAR

LEG TO
SUPPORT THE
SCREEN

SCREW
TO
LIFT
AND
DROP
SCREEN

REGISTRATION STOPS

RUBBER STOPS

BASEBOARD

PRINTING
PAPER

LETTER 'O'
BLOCKED OUT

BASEBOARD

CARD
TO HELP
"SNAP OFF"

SELLOTAPE OR SCOTCH TAPE

CARDBOARD

SECTION THROUGH SQUEEGEE

TWO METHODS OF REGISTRATION

and broadsheets in large quantities.

It is also possible to print on almost any surface, flat or curved; silk-screen prints can even be made on tables, walls and ceilings. The final advantage of this process lies in the areas that can be printed at one time. We have built a screen measuring 6 feet by 2 feet; in this respect the only limiting factors in a school would be the skill of the carpenter and the presence of two children strong enough to pull such a large squeegee across the mesh.

THE SCREEN AND SQUEEGEE
Screen
This is stretched tightly over the base of a frame made from wood and held in place with drawing pins or staples. It can be made from:
Organdie: This material is inexpensive and readily available from local suppliers. However it does sag with use and is easily damaged.
Bolting silk: This is expensive, strong and can be used many times. It is available from silk-screen suppliers.
Nylon: A tough, firm, strong and relatively expensive material. It can be stretched very tightly over the frame when damp. With care a nylon screen will last for a long time without slackening. It is available from silk-screen suppliers and must be degreased before use. If a screen sags, strips of cardboard can be pushed between the bottom of the frame and the mesh to tighten it up.

When the screen has been stretched in position, strips of tape or gumstrip are stuck round the inside of the screen, as shown in Fig. 92. A double layer of tape must be stuck at the top of the

Left. Fig. 95. 'Rowan Gallery', 1971.
Jack Miller, British, born 1944. Silk-screen with glitter. Photographic techniques can be applied to extend the possibilities of silk-screen printing.
'Rowan Gallery' is an example of a photographic stencil on to which glitter has been stuck when the ink was wet.
Right. Fig. 96. 'T Shirt'.
Flocked silk-screen on to cotton. It is possible to stick materials such as sugar, sawdust, flocking or any small granules on to the print by first screening the image wanted in glue or varnish, then sprinkling the material on to it. A three-dimensional surface is then introduced into the silk-screen print. This aspect has been utilized by industry in the making of flocked wallpapers, clothes and, recently, flocked greetings cards.

screen. This acts as a well for the ink to be poured into.
Squeegee: A rubber blade is clamped between two pieces of wood, with the rubber protruding about 1 inch below the bottom of the clamp.
Baseboard: Any flat unmarked surface such as a table top can be used. If necessary the screen may be attached to a base by hinges, which will make it more stable. A 'floating hinge bar' or adjustable bar to which the screen is attached is easy to make and this enables the height of the screen to be adjusted for printing on thick surfaces. This also helps to keep the image crisp and clean.

MATERIALS AND TOOLS

Screen (See Fig. 92.)
Wood, saw, hammer, nails and glue, (for frame).

Mesh: *cotton organdie, silk bolting-cloth or nylon.*
Gum tape and water sponge. Base board or flat base for printing on. Squeegee. Staple gun or drawing pins.
Stencil
Silk-screen stencil knife or scalpel. Thin paper or news-sheet, tracing paper. Profilm, iron. Candle wax, melted wax, liquid shellac, for use with water-based inks. Gum, gouache paint, for use with oil-based printing ink.
Printing
Glass jars or metal containers, cans. Water- or oil-based inks. Transparent base. Water.

HOW TO MAKE STENCILS

There are many ways of making stencils for screen printing and new ways are constantly being discovered. However, we have

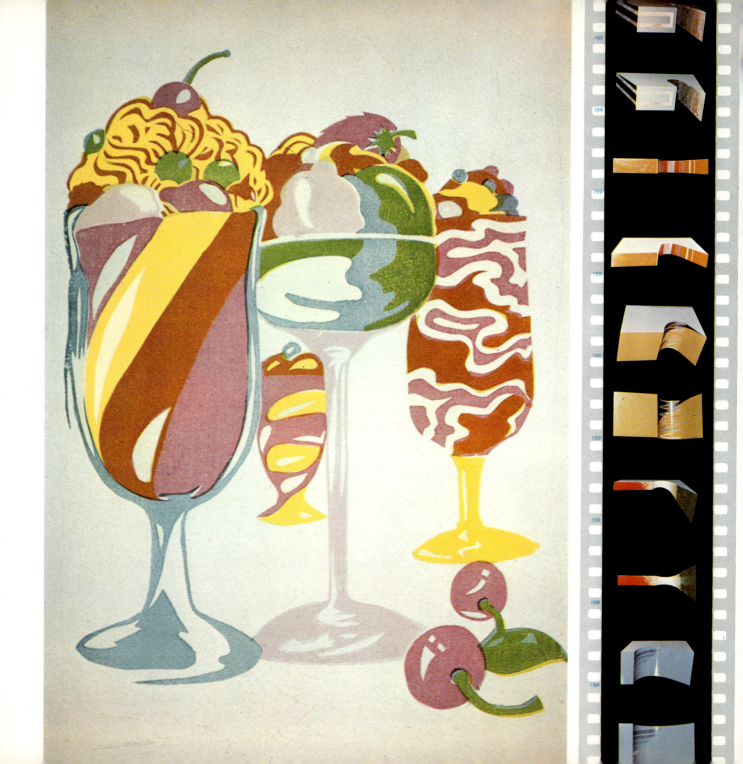

described only four fairly simple
methods which can be used as
starting-points for further
investigation into screen printing.

Film Stencils
These are made from a very thin
sheet of lacquer laminated to
and supported by a backing of
paper or plastic. Probably the
cheapest is Profilm. To make the
stencil all you have to do is to cut
through the top layer of the film
and peel away those parts that you
want to print. Then place the
stencil on a flat surface underneath
the screen and put a layer of
newspaper over the mesh of the
screen as a protection. Press a warm
iron, following the manufacturer's
instructions, firmly on top of the
mesh; this will make the film
adhere to the mesh. You then peel
off the backing sheet and the
remaining film acts as the stencil.

Gum-Resist Stencils
In this method the required image
is drawn directly on to the screen
by means of gum arabic. When the
gum has dried you can print with
oil-based inks. The drawn lines
will appear white on the print. You
can use the gum stencil only with
oil-based inks. If you want to print
with water-based inks you have to
use the reverse principle (i.e. draw
on the screen with oil-based inks).

Tusche
Paint the screen with thick litho
ink, litho chalk or any oil-based
material. When it is dry, coat the
underneath of the screen thinly
with gum, using a piece of cardboard as a squeegee. Allow the gum
coating to dry and then dissolve
the oil-based ink by rubbing with
a cloth and white spirit. The drawn
lines will open and will print. This
is a black-line method.

MIXING OF INKS
Glass jars or tin cans should be
used for mixing ink. For storing
it, lids must be used to exclude air.
If a transparent colour is required,
always add the pigment to the
base. The consistency of the ink
depends on the results required.

The usual consistency for
silk-screen printing can be
compared to thin cream; almost
any thin-consistency ink can be
adapted for silk-screen printing.
For example, poster paint can be
added to the transparent base (e.g.
wallpaper paste).

A slow-drying emulsion paint –
or even gloss paint – can be used
for printing if thinned. It is also
possible to obtain specialist water-
or oil-based inks from manufac-
turers of silk-screen equipment.

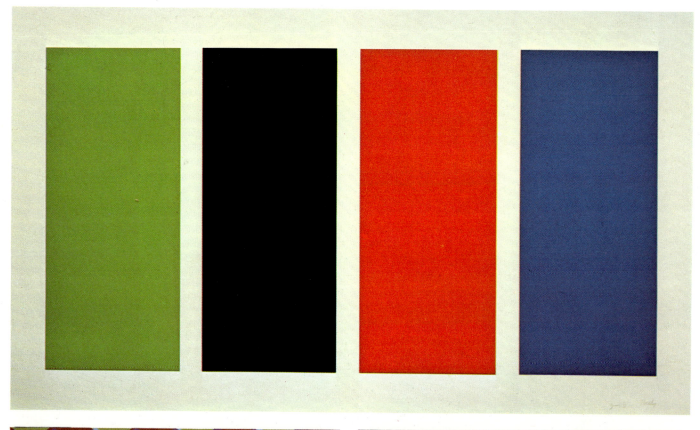

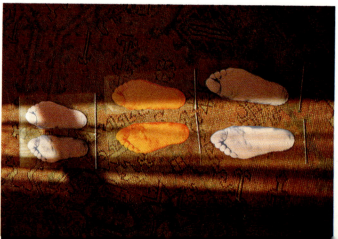

Below. Fig. 103. 'The Great Elvis Presley'. Girl, age 15. Photo silk-screen.

Below and bottom right. Figs. 104–5. Christopher Smith, age 13, making his gum-resist silk-screen print 'Dinosaur' by drawing on to screen with liquid gum arabic. The print is in three colours and was made in one afternoon.

E *

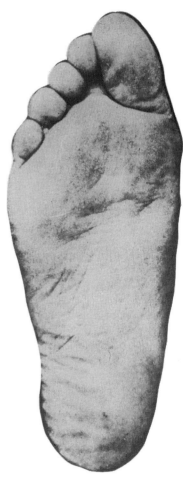

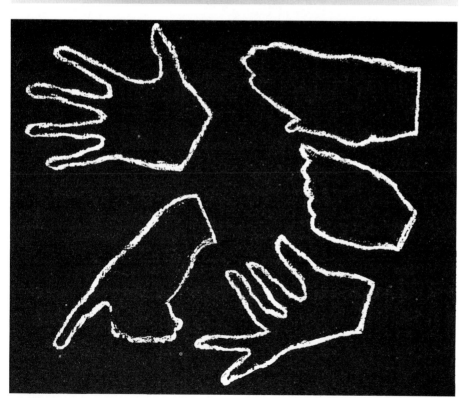

72

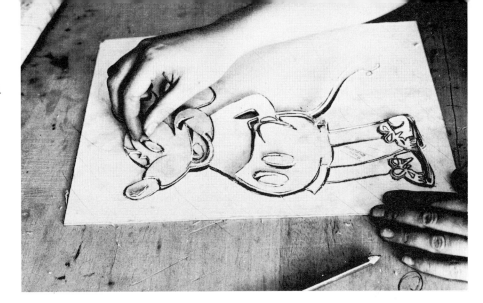

Right. Fig. 109. Mickey Mouse cardboard stencil being assembled uninked.

Below right. Fig. 110. 'Ocean Series IV'. Student. Vacuum-formed printed plastic. A photographic silk-screen of waves was printed on to a flat piece of plastic which was then heated and moulded over a plaster block of the waves in relief. (St. Martin's School of Art, London.)

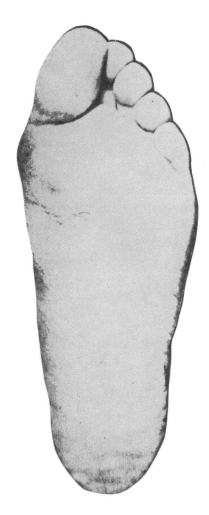

Ocean Series IV 2/6   GR Woolton 1970

Chapter 6
NEW AND
MIXED MEDIA

Left. Fig. 111. Children watching their panoramic print being moved behind an improvised train window.

The advent of photography and the development of a photographic print has made an enormous impact on printmaking, both in relation to the artist and in industry. New processes have been discovered and new machines developed which are expanding and extending the established frontiers of the print into new fields and in new directions. Because of these recent developments in the technological field, simple-to-operate and inexpensive machines have been manufactured, with the result that schools can easily have access to many new and relatively inexpensive methods of making prints.

In this chapter examples of mixed-media prints, not processes, are illustrated and described. Most of the methods, with the exception of photography, have been des-

cribed in detail in this book and in *Simple Printmaking*. The illustrations represent a collection of ideas with reference to the various media and the ways in which both children and artists have translated their thoughts by means of mixed-media prints.

METHODS AND MATERIALS NOT COMMONLY USED IN SCHOOLS

Duplicating machine
It is possible to draw on a duplicating stencil with a hard point or even to type on to one. It can be fed into a duplicating machine or used as a stencil for silk-screen print. Photographic copying machines used for the flat copying of books and dyeline machines will both produce images from three-dimensional objects. (Fig. 29 shows a booklet cover reproduced on a duplicating machine.)

Typewriter
This can be used in many ways to make word pictures and designs (see Figs. 24 and 123).

Canned sprays, air brush, spray gun
Ink or paint is forced out of a small hole when air pressure is released from a container. Ink or paint can be used to spray on, through or round objects, as in stencilling.

Photography
Rayograms or contact prints can be made in the same way as simple stencils. Objects, materials, drawings on acetate, and glass with a black-painted design or magazine pictures can all be held in contact with light-sensitive paper and exposed to a light source. One of the most important new methods to be developed in

Below. Fig. 112. 'Beatles'.
Girl, age 14. This three-dimensional print, produced by relief printing methods, has an apple box stuck on to it to represent the wheels of a train. The Beatles themselves were cut from magazines and stuck on to the print. (Imberhorne Comprehensive School, East Grinstead.)

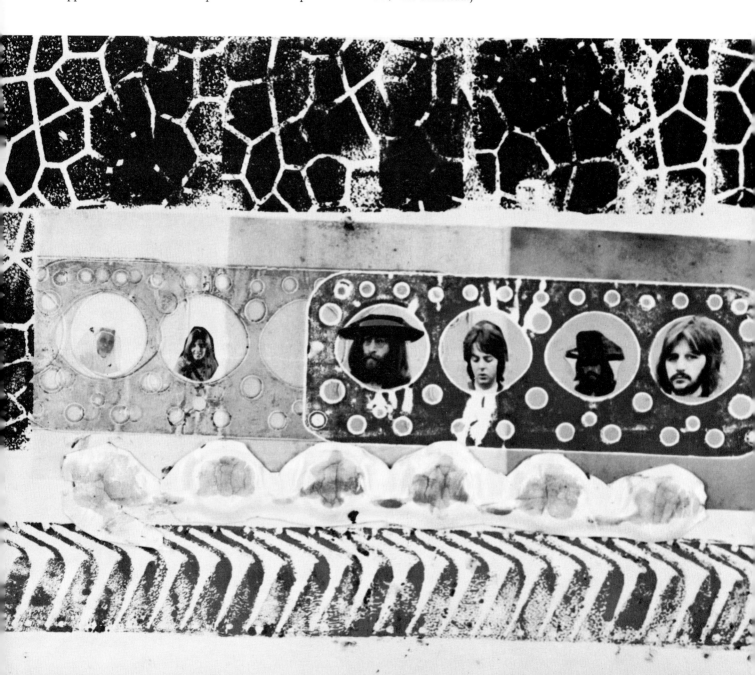

Below. Fig. 113. 'Boy Wonder, Batman'. Michael, age 7. A mixed-media print in which transfer drawing and relief letter blocks are combined. (Saturday morning children's class, Ohio University. Instructor Melody Weiler.)

recent years is photography, plus the related ways of using it, such as photo silk-screen, photo litho or photo etching.

Vacuum-forming

A sheet of plastic is moulded over an object by heat. Although vacuum-forming machines are not normally found in schools, it is possible to take work to a specialist or an art college to be formed. The plastic can either be printed on before forming, or painted, or printed on afterwards.

'This week we did Photograms. It almost had the same principle of the camera. This is the process of a camera. The person taking the picture clicks the clicker. Then puts the film in a chemical. Before they put it in the chemical they expose the film with light after it is in the chemical for a while, they take it out and it's finished.' *Mark Templer, age 8.*

POSTSCRIPT

We hope that it has become apparent from the illustrations shown in both volumes that the print is not always a flat two-dimensional statement. Although we have mentioned vacuum-forming there are very much simpler ways of making a three-dimensional print.

Melody Weiler, a student in the printmaking department at Ohio University, U.S.A. in 1970, ran a class for children on Saturday mornings in the print workshop. Many of the illustrations show work from her classes. With the work she also sent us a synopsis in note form of what she had been doing with the children, part of which is given here. The teachers also included Hugh Kepets and Nancy Dahlstrom:

Fig. 114. 'Frog'.
Girl, age 7. Collage from magazines.
(Redbridge Art Centre.)

Right. Fig. 115. 'Squirrel'.
Child, age 12. Collaged rubbing. (Redbridge
Art Centre.)

The last word

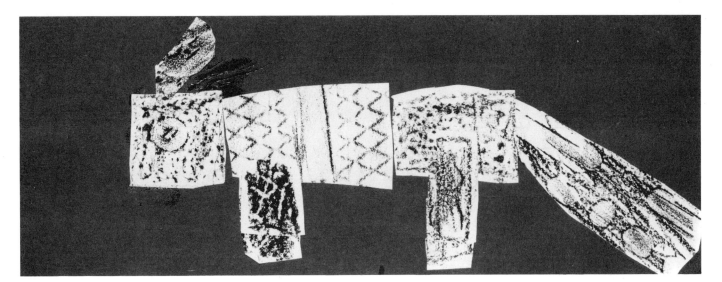

'The first session we made slides. The 35mm paper holders for slides were needed and a variety of materials such as clear acetate which was drawn on with ink, coloured tissue paper, a variety of aggregates such as sand, oil, water, salt, glue. After the window of the slide was covered with clear acetate on both sides, the materials could be laid on top. When their design was finished we ironed the two sides together. Then we had a slide show.'

This project led into photograms.

The children experimented with clear acetate, india ink, black crayons and any objects which were opaque enough to block out the light. Nancy Dahlstrom was in charge of the darkroom. She explained what would happen and how the process resulted. At one time seven kids were in the darkroom, exposing and developing their prints.

They experimented with movement of their hands, overlays of acetate and paper, and the girls used their hair to create some of the images.

After two weeks of photograms we decided to do another play. Gizele brought in the record ''Peter and the Wolf'' and this became the basis of the new play. Hugh pointed out what they could do with a large sheet and an overhead projector and we were able to get some good effects. Everyone took part and Gizele became the director. It was a shadow play. Some of the effects were very exciting. They changed the scenery right before the audience by erasing and re-drawing on the acetate film of the projector.

They did the drawing with magic markers. The costumes were simple, mostly consisting of the children's use of their hands to make a bird's bill, a wolf's mouth or a cat's ear. And that was the culmination of a year's workshop.

It started with my being apprehensive and ended with my being amazed at what I was learning from them. They were their own teachers. Hugh and I were there to encourage and point out different ways and possibilities of working with the different tools and media. From there the children took over, using their own judgement, initiative and imagination to discover and learn for themselves.'

Below. Fig. 118. Child, age 13. Detail of transfer rubbing.

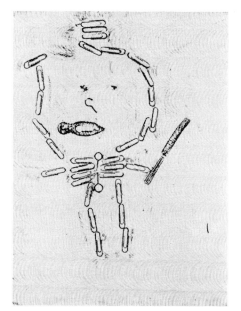

Top left. Fig. 116. Relief print using a piece of cut-out cardboard printed with a merge and combined with numerous printings of a feather to make up the image of a feather duster.

Above left. Fig. 117. 'Mechanical Man'. Patrick, age 5. Rubbing taken on Japanese paper from collograph block.

Above. Fig. 119. 'Playing Cards Series'. Children, age 12. Photograms made by drawing and scraping on to painted acetate (known as *cliché verre*). (Chippenham School. Instructor Wendy Andrews.)

Below. Fig. 120. 'Volkswagen Racing Car'. Bobby Betz III, age 8. Relief and transfer drawing. (Saturday morning children's class, Ohio University. Instructor Melody Weiler.)

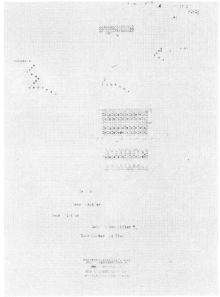

Top right. Fig. 121. Child working on mixed-media print.

Above. Fig. 122. 'Soft Book'. Claes Oldenburg. Silk-screen on plastic.

Above. Fig. 123. 'Typewriter Print'. Anna Hadley, age 12. Here letters and numbers have been used together as an experiment.

Above. Fig. 124. 'Cockscomb'.
John Lord, British, born 1938. Rubber-stamp print and drawing.

Above. Fig. 125. Still-life and prints of various stamping materials.

Below. Fig. 126. 'Women at Curtain'.
Girl, age 14. Collage offset and relief print.
(Imberhorne Comprehensive School, East
Grinstead.)

Below. Fig. 127. 'Shoe'.
Relief prints were taken from all surfaces
of the shoe, and then reconstructed to
form a three-dimensional object.

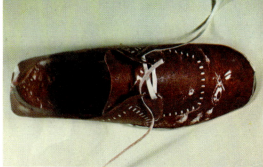

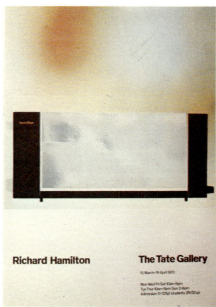

Above. Fig. 128. 'Toaster'.
Richard Hamilton, British, born 1922.
Poster. Offset litho silk-screen and
metalized acetate. (Courtesy of the artist.)

THE ANT STORY

The two blocks I made 4 5
How I made the two blocks 6
The teanniem block I made 8
How I made the teanniem block 8

First I made two blocks. One which had tiny ants (the first one I made) several of them.

Each had six legs, two antennas and som had two pinchers, and every ant hade three sections.

The one for the head was bumpy and ra d. The one for the back and body was a ith orel. The one for the end of the ant wa a bumpyish orel.

There was a bumpy grond with t or three plants with llines represent i the blood vessels.

There were a few birds som which wer taking out worm from the ground. And some we hidd on the tree.

There were some spider webs conecting many of the plants and spide webs had ve many threads. In a few spiderwebs insects w

Finally it started snowing. The ant came back just when it started snowing. A now tlake fit his back and he started owing toward the ant house. Then the daisy star ted daping. Then the ant went in the ant house.

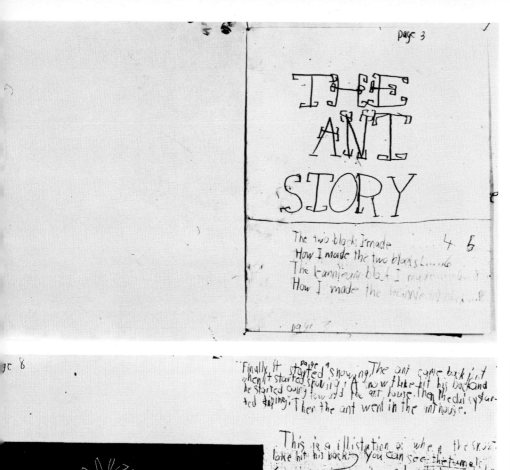

This is a illistation of when the snow lake hit his back. You can see the tunnels underground. I made up how the tunnels look likes.

Leannieam blocks can be very artific. some people are very good at making them. Exspecally people are v.... people are average and beginners like the some people are expert but it is fun for everyone. some prints can be very complicated. And som can have a good amount of lines. And some can even have a few lines.

Leannieam blocks can be almost about anything. A Leannieam block can be print of ants, bookays a flowers, chair, dinosaurs. ect.

First the teacher said to get the pape tols and materail. The he showed us how to h the leannieam block with your left hand (and if you are left handed to use your right hand.) The he showed us how to draw. First get your hand with the knuckles on top then push strai or wiggley. but turn your block if you want to go sideways.

THE END

by Mark Templer
(No middle named)
Nicknam Marco Templer

Figs. 129–33. 'Ant Story'.
Part of a project in which a child wrote a story and illustrated it, attempting to show his past and present work. (See Fig. 75.)

caught in them. page 5

The second one which was the worst one ['made'] because I had rushed on it. It was the one I didn't like because it was very slupy

The second one had only two ants which were very big each was like this: height: 2¾ inches left 2½ inches. They were very harry. With two harry anticnas, six harry legs and two harry pinchers.

The second had a very bumpy ground with a giant house; height: 5½ length x 3½ inches with some palm trees

(I did not like the second block because I rushed alot. wanted it to be bad and was very nervous) I thought it was very horrible and that is why I don't like it.

page 5

First I drew my pictures with grease crayons or I could have drew my pictures with a grease print.

Then I put on some white powder. After that I wiped the extra powder off. Then I put on some goldish powder. Then I wiped off the extra powder.

Then I put on a chemical called gum[?] then I pushed it with my hands with the gum always ahead of my fingers. Then I wiped off the extra gum. And wet the back so the block wouldn't stick to any thing.

Capture 2

The print on the page after the next page is a leannieam block print. It is one of the many living[?] kind of print there are. The leannieam block print is one of the easy ways to make prints.

A leannieam block print may use more than one because a leannieam block may have to have thin lines, thin tones and ball shaped circles. There are shapes for a leannieam block tool a V line and a U

page 6 if on 0.

Your prints with a leannieam block may be good or they may be bad. It depends how you do your print. If you rub hard on the back of your paper it will come out or if you put it in a printing ma[chine] But if you don't rub hard enough it will not turn out well. Or if you move the paper it will not turn out well.

The print on the leannieam block is about an ant. It is true. It once happened in Bloomington, Indiana. It was a poor ant because all the other ants [?] him. And one day he was lost (I knew he was the only ant the other ants fought and I didn't see the ants fighting with an[t]) He was lost for several days. Now there is more ant houses in our yard but a daisy near the ant house of the ant[?]

page 7

This is a picture of my practise leannieam block

Right. Fig. 134. A description of the way the 'Dinosaur' print was made. (See Fig. 75.)

Now we made another print block It is of dinosaurs. The last one we made was [most]ly full of ants. The one we made now might be a little better than the last giant block.

The one we made now everybody that was here helped on it. I think that the one we made now was a little bit more fun to make than the last one.

The one we made now had stegasauruses, brontosauruses, tyrantosaurus, people and giant insects (which I made) such as giant dragonflys and ants. Some other people made giant ferns.

Story by Mark Templer
Block by Mark Templer,
Ronald Earl[?],
Michael [?]
Michael Snavely[?]
Bobby Kek the III

EQUIPMENT AND SUPPLIERS

Most of the firms listed below supply other materials.

PRESSES

Relief Presses:

Graphic Chemical and Ink Co.,
728, North Yale Avenue,
Villa Park, Illinois. 60181.
Area code 312 8326004.
(Dickerson Combination Press,
Combined Etching and Litho Press.)

Harry F. Rochat, A.M.Inst.B.E.,
Cotswold Lodge,
Stapylton Road,
Barnet, Herts.
(Printers' engineers. Suppliers of second-hand presses, reserviced.)

Lithographic Presses:

Charles Brand,
84 East 10th Street,
New York N.Y., 10003.
(Custom built etching and litho presses.)

Hunter, Penrose, Littlejohn Ltd.,
7 Spa Road,
Bermondsey, London, S.E.16.

Etching Presses:

Charles Brand,
84 East 10th Street,
New York N.Y., 10003.
(Custom built etching and litho presses.)

Argus Engineering,
24, King's Bench Street,
London, S.E.1.

Silk-screen Machinery:

Inko Screen Process Supplies Mfg. Co.,
1199 East 12th Street,
Oakland California.

Process Supply Company,
726 Hanley Industrial Court,
Saint Louis,
Missouri, 63144,
(Silk-screen materials.)

TOOLS AND EQUIPMENT

Relief equipment. General suppliers of cutting tools, blocks and other equipment.

The Craftool Company,
1 Industrial Road,
Wood-Ridge,
New Jersey, 07075.
(All printmaker's materials.)

T. N. Lawrence & Sons Ltd.,
2–4 Bleeding Heart Yard,
Greville Street,
Hatton Garden,
London, E.C.1.
(Papers, wood blocks, and cutting tools.)

Alec Tiranti Ltd.,
72 Charlotte Street,
London, W.1.
(Artists' materials for printmakers, especially wood cutting tools.)

Dunlop Chemical Products
Division,
Chester Road Factory,
Birmingham 24.
(Dunlop Latex Compounds.)

Unibond Products,
Camberley, Surrey.
(P.V.A. adhesive.)

General Litho Equipment:
W. R. Grace & Co.,
21–24 Thirty-Ninth Avenue,
Long Island City,
New York, 11101.
(Lithographic rollers and other
materials.)

Algraphy Ltd.,
Murray Road,
Orpington, Kent BR5 3QR.
(Lithographic supplies and
servicing.)

Hunter, Penrose, Littlejohn Ltd.,
7 Spa Road,
Bermondsey, London, S.E.16.

General Etching Equipment:
Cronite Co. Inc.,
Kennedy Boulevard at 88th Street,
North Bergen, New Jersey.
(Etching materials, inks.)

W. C. Kimber Successors Ltd.,
24 King's Bench Street,
London, S.E.1.

F. Charbonnel,
13, Quai Montebello,
Paris – V^e. France.

Etching Blankets:
Continental Felt Company,
22–26 West 15th Street,
New York, II. N.Y.
(Etching blankets and other felts.)

Aetna Felt Co., Inc.,
204 Center Street,
New York, N.Y.

Thomas Hardman & Sons Ltd.,
Fernhill Mills,
Bury, Lancs.

Etching Acid Baths:
Peerless Camera Stores,
415 Lexington Avenue,
New York, N.Y.

Hunter, Penrose, Littlejohn Ltd.,
7 Spa Road,
Bermondsey, London, S.E.16.

Etching Plates:
National Steel & Copper,
700 South Clinton Street,
Chicago, Illinois.

S.P. Syndicate,
121, Westminster Bridge Road,
London, S.E.1.

Silk-screen General Equipment:
Becker Sign Supply Co.,
319–321 N. Paca Street,
Baltimore 1.

Serascreen Corporation,
147 West 15 Street,
New York II.

E. T. Marler Ltd.,
191 Western Road,
Merton Abbey,
London, S.W.19.

Samco – Strong Ltd.,
Clayhill,
Bristol, BS99 7ER.

Geliot Whitman Ltd.,
16a Herschell Road,
Brockley Rise,
London, S.E.23.
(Plan chests, general artists'
materials.)

INKS

Relief Printing Inks:

Cronite Co., Inc.,
35, Park Place,
New York. N.Y.

California Ink Co.,
2939, East Piko Boulevard,
Los Angeles 23, California.

A. Gilbey & Son,
Reliance Works,
Devonshire Road,
Colliers Wood,
London, S.W.19.

Winstones,
150 Clerkenwell Road,
London, E.C.1.

Litho Ink:

Graphic Chemical and Ink Co.,
728, North Yale Avenue,
Villa Park,
Illinois, 60181.
Area code 312 8326004.

Manders-Kidd Ltd.,
St. Johns Street,
Wolverhampton, England.

Etching Inks:

Interchemical Corp.,
Printing Ink Division,
175 Albany Street,
Cambridge 39, Mass.

Lorilleux-Lefranc & Co.,
16, Rue Suger,
Paris VIe.

Silk-screen Inks:

Interchemical Printing Ink
Corporation,
67 West 44 Street,
New York.

Selectasine Silk Screens Ltd.,
22 Bulstrode Street,
London, W.1.

Sericol,
24 Parsons Green Lane,
London, S.W.6.

John T. Keep & Sons Ltd.,
15 Theobalds Road,
London, W.C.1.

(Water-based):

W. M. McReary,
815 Lisbon Road,
Belfast,
Northern Ireland. 07979X.

Rollers: Relief Printing, Gelatine, Rubber, Plastic:

Apex Printers Roller Company,
1541 North 16th Street,
St. Louis 6, Missouri,
(Rollers, gelatine, plastic, rubber, all sizes.)

T. N. Lawrence & Son Ltd.,
2–4 Bleeding Heart Yard,
Greville Street,
Hatton Garden,
London, E.C. 1.

Lithographic Rollers, Nap, offset and composition:

W. R. Grace & Co.,
21–24 Thirty-Ninth Avenue,
Long Island City,
New York 11101.
(Ideal Roller.)

Ault & Wiborg, Ltd.,
Stander Road,
Smithfields,
London, S.W. 18.

Etching Rollers:

Apex Printers Rollers Company,
1541 North 16th Street,
St. Louis 6, Missouri.

Hunter, Penrose, Littlejohn Ltd.,
7 Spa Road,
Bermondsey, London, S.E.16.

PAPERS

Relief Papers Japanese:

Andrews, Nelson & Whitehead,
Boise Cascade Corporation,
7 Laight Street,
New York, N.Y. 10013.
(Printing Papers.)

T. N. Lawrence & Son Ltd.,
2–4 Bleeding Heart Yard,
Greville Street,
Hatton Garden,
London, E.C.1.
(Imitation, and Japanese Papers.)

John Dickinson,
35 Newbridge Street,
London, E.C.4.

Newssheet and other cheap papers—
Local Suppliers.

Yamada Shokai Co. Ltd.,
5 5 Yasu, Chuo-Ku,
Tokyo, Japan.
(Hand-made printing papers.)

Arjomari-Prioux,
3 rue du Pont-de Lodi,
Paris 6, France.
(Printing papers, Ingres, Rives, etc.)

Lithographic Papers:

R. K. Burt & Co. Ltd.,
38 Farrington Street,
London, E.C.4.
(Hand-made and mould-made papers.)

GLOSSARY

Etching Papers:

W. & R. Balston Ltd.,
Springfield Mill,
Maidstone, Kent.
(Makers of hand-made, mould-
made and filter papers.)

Silk-screen Papers:

Technical Paper Corp.,
25, Huntingdon Avenue,
Boston, 16. Mass.

General Suppliers:

Reeves & Sons Ltd.,
Enfield, Middlesex.

Rowney & Co. Ltd.,
11, Pevey Street,
London, W.1.

Winsor & Newton,
51 Rathbone Place,
London, W.1.
(Also paper lithoplates.)

Asphaltum. A greasy liquid which may be used as a resist in intaglio. Also used in lithography for drawing and processing.
Baren. Traditionally Japanese, a slightly convex hand tool for burnishing paper.
Blankets. Felt used in printing intaglio; also the rubberized covering on the cylinder of an offset litho press.
Blind printing. (See embossing.)
Brayer or roller. Hand roller made in rubber, plastic or gelatine, for inking blocks and plates.
Burin or graver. An engraving tool with either a square or a lozenge-shaped metal shaft.
Burnisher. Metal tool used for polishing metal plates.
Cardboard. A smooth white board.
Cliché Verre. A print made on photographic paper by drawing and scraping on to coated glass.

Collage. Sticking objects, paper etc. on to a background.

Collograph. A block made from objects and textures glued to a surface.

Decalcomania. A mirror image produced by folding a piece of paper covered with wet paint or ink and then pulling it apart. (Double decalcomania: the same process repeated on the same print.)

Draw tool. Tool used for cutting metal.

Drypoint. Scratches made directly on to metal, creating a burr which has a soft velvety look when printed in intaglio.

Embossing. Also known as gauffrage or Kara-zuri. Printing from uninked blocks or plates which gives a three-dimensional form.

End-grain. Block for wood engraving, fashioned from the end-grain of wood.

Etching ground. An acid-resist, coated or rolled on to the surface of the plate. Soft ground: for impressing textures to be etched in the metal. Hard ground: to be drawn into with a sharp point.

Etching needle. A steel point used to draw the design on to the resist-covered metal.

Etching or biting. Eating into a metal plate with acid.

Frottage. Direct print made from surfaces by rubbing.

Glue block. Block made from thick glue on a base.

Graver. (See Burin.)

Heelball. Hard wax widely used for taking rubbings.

Impression. A print taken by any method.

Intaglio. A print taken from indentations below the surface of the block or plate.

Jig or bench hook. Wooden device on which lino rests when cutting.

Key drawing. The master drawing (see registration).

Letterpress. A method of printing from type high relief blocks.

Lino cut. Linoleum gouged, cut and printed in relief.

Lithographic crayon. Usually known as chalk, for drawing on litho stones and plates.

Lithography. A planographic (flat) process for producing prints.

Litmask. Paper stencil used on offset litho machines.

Marbling. A print taken from oil-bound inks floating on water.

Merge. (See Rainbow printing.)

Monoprint. A 'one-off' print which cannot be repeated.

Monotype. (See Monoprint.)

Nitric acid. Used for etching metal plates.

Offset. A transfer from one surface to another.

Plank wood. The material used for woodcuts, the grain runs across the surface of the block.

Planographic. Printed from a flat surface (i.e. lithography, screen printing).

Plexiglass. A plastic also known as lucite, which can be used in intaglio printing.

Proof. A print taken before work on the block or plate has finished.

Rainbow printing or merge. Separate colours, blending smoothly together, made with a roller.

Registration. The required positioning of block and paper.

Relief print. A print taken from the top surface of a relief block.

Resist. Liquid applied to parts of a metal plate to prevent acid biting them.

Roller offset. A print made with a composition roller. (See offset.)

Roller stencilling. Stencil printed with a composition roller.

Rubbing. (See Frottage.)

Scraper. Part of a lithographic press, usually a wooden bar covered with leather.

Scrim. Cloth used for wiping surplus ink from a plate, also called tarlatan or cheesecloth.

Silk-screen. Mesh stretched over a wooden frame.

Splattering. The flickering of ink on to printing paper with a brush.

Stencil. Perforated material over which ink is rolled, dabbed, or pulled.

Stippling. The dabbing with a brush to make a textured surface.

Stop-out varnish. Acid resist.

Squeegee. A strip of rubber clamped between wood, used to draw ink across the screen when printing.

Transfer drawing. A print made by pressure on to the back of paper placed face down on an inked slab.

Transparent base. A base used for carrying pigment, used to improve transparency, e.g. wallpaper paste.

Tusche. Liquid ink; grease.

Woodcut. Plank wood cut with gouges or knives, printed in relief.

Wood engraving. A delicate engraving process on end-grain wood.

BIBLIOGRAPHY

GENERAL

American Printmaking 1670–1965.
In *Art in America*.
July-August Issue, Art in
America Co. Inc. New York.

Brunner, Felix.
*A Handbook of Graphic
Reproduction Processes*.
Alec Tiranti Ltd., London, 1962.

Daniels, Harvey.
Printmaking.
Paul Hamlyn 1971.

Erickson, Janet Doub, and
Sproul Adelaide.
Printmaking without a Press.
Reinhold Publishing Corporation,
New York, 1966.

Ernst, Max.
Beyond Painting.
Wittenbern, Schultz Inc., New
York, 1948.

Hayter, S. W.
About Prints.
Oxford University Press, 1962.

Heller, Jules.
Printmaking Today.
Holt, Rinehard, Winston, 1966.

Ivins, Jnr., William, M.
Print and Visual Communication.
Da Capo Press Series in Graphic
Art 1969. General Editor
A. Hyatt Mayor.

Peterdi, Gabor.
Printmaking.
Macmillan Co., New York, 1959.

Rasmusen, Henry.
Printmaking with Monotype.
Chilton Company, New York,
1960.

Sotriffer, Kristian.
*Printmaking History and
Technique*.
Thames and Hudson, 1968.

Stubbe, Wolf.
History of Modern Graphic Art.
Thames and Hudson, 1963.

Wechsler, Herman J.
  Great Prints and Printmakers.
  Thames and Hudson, 1967.
Zigrosser, Carl.
  The Book of Fine Prints.
  Crown Publishers Inc., New
  York, 1958.

SILK-SCREEN
Carr, Francis.
  *A Guide to Screen Process
  Printing.*
  Vista Books, London, 1961.
Fossett, Robert O.
  *Techniques in Photography for the
  Silk-Screen Printer.*
  Signs of the Times Publishing
  Co., Ohio, 1959.
Kosloff, Albert.
  Screen Process Printing.
  Signs of the Times Publishing
  Co., Ohio, 1950.

Russ, Stephen.
  *A Guide to Practical Silk-screen
  Printing.*
  Studio Vista, 1971.
Shokler, Harry.
  *Artists' Manual for Silk-screen
  Printmaking.*
  Tudor Publishing Co., New
  York, 1960.

RELIEF PRINTING
Biggs, John R.
  Woodcuts.
  Blandford Press, London, 1958.
Gorbaty, Norman.
  Printmaking with a Spoon.
  Reinhold, New York, 1960.
Green, Peter.
  Creative Printmaking.
  B. J. Batsford Ltd., London,
  1964.

Hasuda, Yojuro, Editor.
  Shiko Munakata.
  Kodansha Library of Japanese
  Art No. 12.
  English Text by Oliver Statler.
  Charles E. Tuttle Co., 1958.
Rothenstein, Michael.
  Frontiers of Printmaking.
  Studio Vista, 1966.
Rothenstein, Michael.
  Linocuts and Woodcuts.
  Studio Books, 1962.
Rothenstein, Michael.
  Relief Printing: Basic Methods.
  New Directions.
  Studio Vista, 1970.

ETCHING
Gross, Anthony.
  *Etching, Engraving, and Intaglio
  Printing.*
  Oxford University Press, London.
  New York, Toronto, 1970.

Hayter, S. W.
New Ways of Gravure.
Oxford University Press, London,
1966.

Hind, A. M.
History of Engraving.
Dover Publications. New York,
1963.

Lumsdon, Ernest.
The Art of Etching.
Seeley, Service and Co., London,
1962.

Short, Frank.
On the Making of Etchings
(Robert Dunthorne, At the Sign
of Rembrandt's Head, Vigo
Street, London, 1888).

Trevelyan, Julian.
Etching.
Studio Handbook, London, 1963.

LITHOGRAPHY

Cliffe, Henry.
Lithography.
Studio Vista.

Jones, Stanley.
Lithography for Artists.
Oxford Paperbacks, Handbooks
for Artists.

Knigin, Michael, and Murray
Zimiles.
*The Technique of Fine Art
Lithography.*
Van Nostrand Reinhold, 1970.

Man, Felix.
150 Years of Artists' Lithographs.
London, 1953.

Trivick, Henry.
Auto-Lithography.
Faber and Faber, 1960.

Weber, W.
History of Lithography.
Thames and Hudson, 1966.